THE GARDEN IN
100
OBJECTS

THE GARDEN IN
100
OBJECTS

From the iconic to the rare
at the Missouri Botanical Garden

Published in the U.S. by:

Missouri Botanical Garden

P.O. Box 299

St. Louis, MO 63166-0299

www.mobot.org

ISBN 978-0-9884551-3-9

Cataloging-in-Publication Data available upon request.

1 2 3 4 5 04 05 06 07 08

Writer: Elizabeth McNulty

Editor: Liz Fathman

Designer: Jeffrey Ricker

Photographers: Ryan Lay and Kat Niehaus. Additional photography by
Sonya Buerck, Kent Burgess, Christopher Gibbons, Brent Johnston, J. J. Mueller, Josh Nezam, Benjamin Staver, and Laila Wessel.

Printer: Cenveo, Inc

Many Garden staff contributed to this book. Thanks to: Wendy Applequist, John Behrer, Paul Brockmann, Kate Brueggemann, Rainer Bussmann, Vickie Campbell, Ben Chu, Andrew Colligan, Thomas Croat, Gerrit Davidse, Jason Delaney, Heidi Dowgwillo, Kathy Farris, Liz Fathman, Ellen Flesch, Lisa Francis, Katherine Freeman, Robbie Hart, Donna Herrera, Doug Holland, June Hutson, Allison Jones, Glenn Kopp, Deborah Lalumondier, Peggy Lents, Bob Magill, Kevin Mattingly, Donna McGinnis, James Miller, Tyler Nowell, Linda Oestry, Rosa Ortiz-Gentry, Jan Salick, Jennifer Smith, Steve Smith, Jim Soloman, Rebecca Sucher, Marcie Touchette, Lydia Toth, James Trager, Carmen Ulloa, Sheila Voss, Blanche Wagner, Darman Williams, Jennifer Wolff, Steve Wolff, Scott Woodbury, Bob Woodruff, Andrew Wyatt, and Peter Wyse Jackson.

CONTENTS

YATSUHASHI (ZIGZAG) BRIDGE
in the Japanese Garden, see
page 21.

INTRODUCTION

It is enriching for all of us to be part of an institution that has such a remarkable and diverse history, where our present, and our future, is shaped so fundamentally by what has come before us. Everywhere I go in the Garden, every door I pass through, every path I walk, every drawer I open, every book I examine tells a story of the people, priorities, and aspirations that have shaped this great Garden. We can understand our own tasks as stewards of the Missouri Botanical Garden so much better when we know and cherish what has come before us. There's a thrill in contemplating, for example, that Charles Darwin himself once held this little fern, now dried, in his hand (page 44). Or that Henry Shaw used this very key to unlock his wine cellar (page 18). Objects help bring history to life.

Some objects can hold mysteries. Why should we care about this modest handwritten slip of paper (page 113)? It turns out that this is a receipt that represents the beginning of the Missouri Botanical Garden Herbarium, which is today one of the largest and finest such research facilities in the world. Another unusual item is a clunky old computer (page 93). In the early 1980s, this computer launched Tropicos, the world's first botanical database. Thus began the current digital era and exponential leaps in our connectivity and collaboration with botanical institutions around the globe.

At a botanical garden, the objects we study can be living objects: plants. The large specimen of *Dracaena umbraculifera* in the Climatron was thought extinct in the wild until recently when it was rediscovered by our scientists after more than 200 years (page 70). The water lilies (page 66) tell the story of the Missouri Botanical Garden's famed breeding program in the early 20th century. The Last Rose of Summer (page 126) is a more recent tale: I brought it to St. Louis from my mother's garden in Ireland.

Dr. Peter Wyse Jackson with one of his old friends, *Hyophorbe lagenicaulis* or the Round Island bottle palm. See page 91.

Whether it's the largest seed in the plant kingdom (page 100) or the oldest book in our library (page 96), I hope you'll find the stories behind these objects the fascinating beginning of a conversation about where we have come from and why what we do today will shape the important future of the Missouri Botanical Garden as one of the world's great environmental leaders.

Dr. Peter Wyse Jackson
President, Missouri Botanical Garden

The genesis of the mark is the folk symbol for human.

 Compounded to become humans (humankind) abstracted to become plant form (botanical). Reflecting the Garden's dual concerns for humans and the natural world. The inseparable nature of both and, most importantly, their "oneness."

Also the process of research.

 A seed pod.

 Germinating. Seeking the common denominator in the plant kingdom, the point at which most things look alike, so as to represent the entire kingdom and not one part…newness…growth.

 The two forms brought together…and divided, symbolizing in their separateness plant and human, in their symmetry or reflection, the interdependence of one upon the other to create a whole, a mutual reinforcement. Again, "oneness."

 The curved lower line: the garden as holding, cradling, nurturing the whole: the Earth.

Symbol designed and explicated by Chip Reay of Hellmuth, Obata, and Kassabaum, Inc. in 1972.

IN 1829 DR. NATHANIEL Bagshaw Ward of London accidentally created a garden in a sealed jar. An early version of the terrarium, the Wardian case quickly became a stylish feature of Victorian drawing rooms on both sides of the Atlantic. It revolutionized the commercial viability of tropical plants. Most importantly, the Wardian case allowed plant scientists to ship living specimens back to research facilities, including the Missouri Botanical Garden.

AN ALOE THE SIZE OF A TREE, *ALOE dichotoma* is called African Quiver tree because the San people use its tubular branches to make quivers. The trees grow in Namibia and South Africa, but are threatened due to global climate change. (opposite)

THE GARDEN IN 100 OBJECTS

THE CENTERPIECE OF THE
George Washington Carver
Garden is this life-sized
bronze by acclaimed African-
American sculptor Tina
Allen. Wearing a wise, gentle
expression, Carver holds an
amaryllis flower to the light.
Carver hybridized amaryllis
as a hobby, but he is perhaps
best known for his pioneering
agricultural research and his
work to educate and elevate
poor Southern farmers.
He was born into slavery in
Missouri, but died in 1943 a
hero of the nation.

HUMANS AREN'T THE ONLY ANIMALS THAT ENJOY THE Garden. Would you believe…red fox families, murders of crows, mama 'possums, raccoons (inside and out), turtles, fish, frogs, toads, lizards, snakes, chipmunks, mice, deer, dogs, cats, birds of many kinds, and squirrels, squirrels, squirrels, squirrels, squirrels!

THE "WIDOWMAKER," AS IT IS sometimes known. Cones of the Coulter pine (*Pinus coulterii*) can be 16 inches long and weigh 10 pounds (shown here with pine cones from the *Pinus echinata*, short-leaf pine, the only pine native to Missouri). People working in Coulter pine groves are advised to wear hardhats. The species grows in the coastal mountains of Southern California and northern Baja California, Mexico, and is named for Thomas Coulter, an Irish botanist who conducted research there in the early 1800s. The Garden's current president, Dr. Peter Wyse Jackson, keeps this cone in his office. A native of Ireland, he attended Trinity College, Dublin, where Coulter founded the herbarium.

INSIDE THE SHOENBERG Temperate House. The antique portico overlooking the Moorish garden was once the façade of a Catholic school near 23rd and Mullanphy streets in St. Louis. Built in 1903, St. Leo's School was designed by the sons of George I. Barnett, the famed 19th-century architect who designed several historical buildings on the Garden grounds. When the school was demolished in 1978, the Garden bought the portico.

She is Venus when she smiles
But she's Juno when she walks.

–Ben Jonson

COPY OF THE FARNESE
Juno (Naples). Originally she
stood in a formal garden
near where Gladney Rose
Garden is now. Despite her
four-ton weight, she has
been moved several times
in the history of the Garden.

The deep wine
of it risen tall above
the buried
corm,

its ornamental
spathe furrowed
thoughtfully, to
human warmth.

…

with its allure
of rotting flesh
for the scarabs
to follow,

…

Call it life
enrapt with death's
blight, blooming
briefly.

–excerpt from "Corpse Flower, Luna Moth"
by Daniel Tobin

CORPSE FLOWER (*AMORPHOPHALLUS titanum*) on display in the Linnean House.

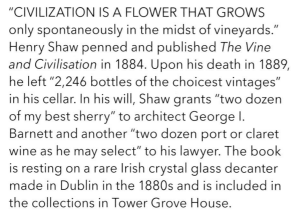

"CIVILIZATION IS A FLOWER THAT GROWS only spontaneously in the midst of vineyards." Henry Shaw penned and published *The Vine and Civilisation* in 1884. Upon his death in 1889, he left "2,246 bottles of the choicest vintages" in his cellar. In his will, Shaw grants "two dozen of my best sherry" to architect George I. Barnett and another "two dozen port or claret wine as he may select" to his lawyer. The book is resting on a rare Irish crystal glass decanter made in Dublin in the 1880s and is included in the collections in Tower Grove House.

THIS CHARMING BUILDING IN THE Georgian style is emblazoned "Botanical Museum and Library. Founded 1859." Though it was not completed until 1860, it did indeed house a natural history collection, including plants, fossils, and taxidermied birds and animals, as well as the original library and herbarium. The Garden's scientific endeavors outgrew the facility, and it closed to the public in 1982. After 30 years, thanks to the *Garden for the World* campaign, it is slated for renovation and reopening.

EXILED FROM KYOTO AFTER an affair with a high-ranking court lady, Ise stops at Yatsuhashi, a place where a stream branches into eight channels, each with its own bridge. The sight of irises prompts him to compose a nostalgic love poem:

I wear robes with well-worn
   hems,
Reminding me of my dear wife
I fondly think of always,
So as my sojourn stretches on
   tabi
Ever farther from home,
Sadness fills my thoughts.

*—Tales of Ise (circa 900 CE),
translated from the Japanese
by John T. Carpenter*

YATSUHASHI (ZIGZAG) BRIDGE
in the Japanese Garden.

SHAW BEGAN HIS LIBRARY WITH A SMALL COLLECTION OF books. Add to this the Engelmann and Sturtevant gifts, and a research facility was born. Today, the Peter H. Raven Library is one of the world's premier botanical libraries with over 200,000 volumes and 6,500 rare books.

IRIS WAS THE GREEK GODDESS OF THE rainbow. The Alice Hahn Goodman Iris Garden is playfully designed in the shape of a rainbow and features a rainbow of colors as well. The symbol of St. Louis's French history, the fleur-de-lis, as seen on the City flag, is in fact a stylized iris. (opposite)

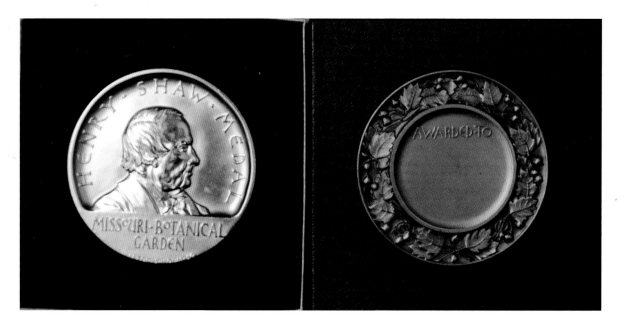

THE HENRY SHAW MEDAL HAS BEEN AWARDED
since 1893. It honors those who have made a
significant contribution to the Missouri Botanical
Garden, botanical research, horticulture,
conservation, or the museum community.

Because I could not stop for Death,

He kindly stopped for me.

—Emily Dickinson

THE BODY OF HENRY SHAW, DEAD AT THE AGE OF 89, LYING
in state in the Museum Building in August 1889. The mayor of
St. Louis ordered a period of mourning in the city until after
the funeral. Flags flew at half-mast. Mourners entered the
Museum from the front entrance to pay their last respects.
Shaw was then moved to his final resting place, his mausoleum
on Garden grounds.

RED-EARED SLIDERS IN THE JAPANESE GARDEN. THE TURTLE
is a symbol of longevity and happiness in Japan. A quasi-
mythical giant turtle, the *minogame*, is widely depicted in
Japanese arts and crafts with what appears to be a long hairy
tail! In fact, the "tail" is seaweed that has grown on the turtle's
shell due to its immense age.

NELUMBO NUCIFERA (SACRED LOTUS) IS A RHIZOMATOUS AQUATIC
perennial found in the margins of pools of southern Asia. It is sacred in Buddhism,
a symbol of purity, arising from the mud to unfurl a pure white or blushing pink
bloom. Its brevity of flowering, a mere day or two, suggests the transitory nature
of this world. The seeds, however, can live for centuries. Radiocarbon dating has
determined the age of the oldest known germinating seed to be approximately
1,200 years. (opposite)

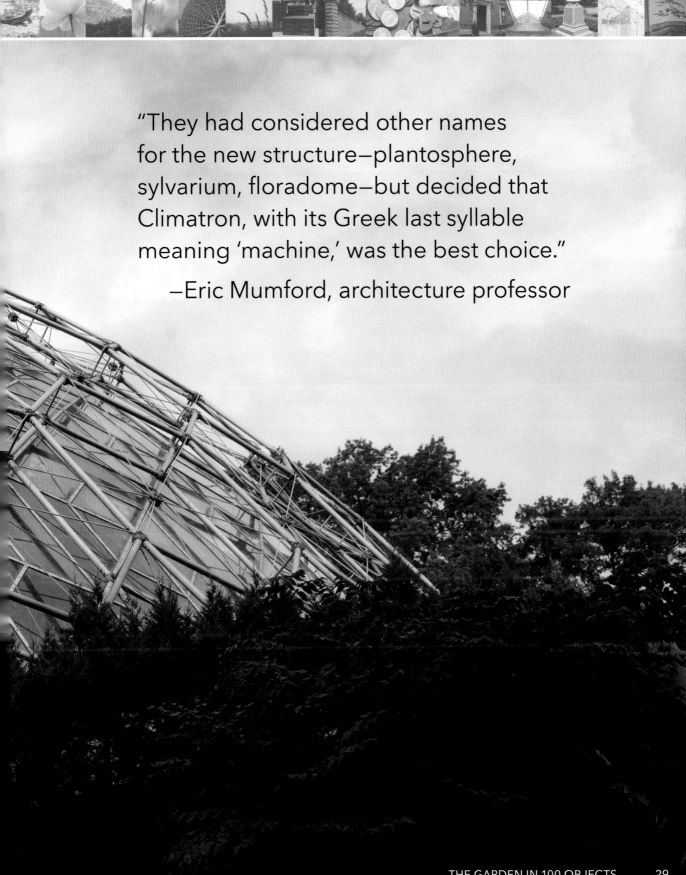

"They had considered other names for the new structure—plantosphere, sylvarium, floradome—but decided that Climatron, with its Greek last syllable meaning 'machine,' was the best choice."

—Eric Mumford, architecture professor

INSPIRED BY THE BAVARIAN ALPS, THE ALPINE plants growing in the Floyd Pfautch Bavarian Garden represent many different high-altitude regions, including Finland, Switzerland, France, Spain, Tibet, and others. Alpine regions are one of the most vulnerable to climate change. As temperatures warm, specially adapted plants must migrate up the mountain to cooler climes in order to survive.

BOTTOM OF A *VICTORIA* LILY. SHAW'S first head gardener James Gurney worked with *Victoria* lilies as a young man at the Royal Botanic Gardens, Kew, where he once presented the flower to Queen Victoria. In the 1890s, Gurney introduced the showstopper to both the Garden and Tower Grove Park. Many photo ops ensued with ladies perched on hidden platforms topped by *Victoria*s. What few people know is that the underside of this gigantic leaf is studded with wicked thorns, all the better to deter would-be herbivores.

"THE PRAIRIE WAS uncultivated, without trees or fences, but covered with tall luxuriant grass, undulated by the gentle breezes of spring." Henry Shaw describes his first view of the land that would become the Missouri Botanical Garden. Prairie once covered much of the central U.S. including nearly half of Missouri. The reconstructed Shaw Nature Reserve prairie provides an idea of what these "oceans" of tall grass were like.

THE *FLORA OF CHINA*. A COMPREHENSIVE CATALOG OF
China's entire 31,500 species, the *Flora of China* is a collaboration
mainly between Chinese and American botanists from the
Missouri Botanical Garden that began informally in the late
1980s. Work was completed on all 44 volumes in 2013. Almost
35 percent of China's flora is known to have been used for their
medicinal properties, one of many reasons a thorough, up-to-
date inventory of the country's flora is so important!

THE 1,000-FOOT-LONG EASTERN BOUNDARY WALL IS MADE
of native limestone and varies from 9 to 12 feet high. When
constructed in the 1850s, there were originally three walls to
shelter tender plants within and to keep out the many animals
that roamed this rural location. In 2013, the Garden received a
Save America's Treasures grant from the U.S. Department of the
Interior to restore and rebuild crumbling sections. (opposite)

CLIMATRON TOKENS, 1960. The Climatron saved the Garden from financial depression. Visitors were required to purchase a 50 cent token, which was then deposited in a turnstile at the entrance. The Climatron brought in $2,000 a week during the first few months it was open in 1960—and doubled the Garden's attendance within the year.

THESE FRENCH IRONS, CLIMBING BICYCLE, AND CLIPPER pole were used by Garden botanist Alwyn Howard Gentry to scale trees and collect plant specimens. Gentry developed a method of transect sampling to quantify species diversity in degrading or disappearing ecosystems. His work would eventually lead to Conservation International's Rapid Assessment Program. Gentry published close to 200 scientific papers and collected nearly 80,000 plant specimens in his lifetime, which was tragically cut short. He died in a plane crash in 1993 while conducting an aerial conservation survey over Ecuador.

SHAW'S TOWN HOUSE ORIGINALLY STOOD in downtown St. Louis at 7th and Locust. Per provisions in his will, the house was to be taken down after his death and reassembled somewhere on his country estate. The exact location was unspecified. His long-time housekeeper, Rebecca Edom, claimed that Shaw came to her in a vision and insisted the house be placed in the southeast corner of the property.

THE ORIGINAL MURAL WAS PAINTED
by Leon Pomarède, the artist who created
several prominent murals in antebellum
St. Louis, including the Old Cathedral,
Mercantile Library Hall, and Saint Louis
University Hall; all since gone. This mural too
is somewhat gone: due to water damage and
age, it was "freshened up" by a different artist
in 1930 (who added the peacocks). The original
glory of the installation will once again be on
display when the Museum Building reopens.

INSTALLED IN 1887 BY SHAW AT THE suggestion of his scientific advisor Engelmann, this pink granite obelisk is "in honour of American Science" and "to the memory Thomas Nuttall." Engelmann deemed Nuttall the "father of western American Botany," but the Garden's first director may have had a differing opinion (at least of the obelisk). Trelease put in a request to have the object moved six feet. When the Trustees asked him in which direction, he is rumored to have replied: "Down."

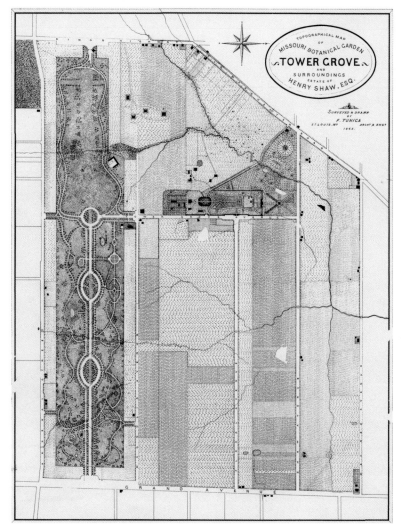

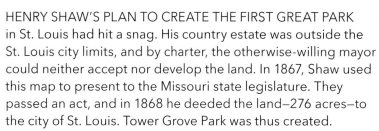

HENRY SHAW'S PLAN TO CREATE THE FIRST GREAT PARK
in St. Louis had hit a snag. His country estate was outside the
St. Louis city limits, and by charter, the otherwise-willing mayor
could neither accept nor develop the land. In 1867, Shaw used
this map to present to the Missouri state legislature. They
passed an act, and in 1868 he deeded the land—276 acres—to
the city of St. Louis. Tower Grove Park was thus created.

A PRE-LINNEAN HERBARIUM FROM THE mid-1700s. The Garden Herbarium is an environmentally stable repository that protects dried plant specimens from fire, insect pests, and other agents of deterioration. Modern specimens have more or less uniform labeling, and through digital technology, are increasingly viewable online.

However, once upon a time, these bundles constituted "an herbarium." Tucked inside are dozens of plant specimens collected for George Boehmer's *Flora Lipsiae indigena* (1750), each with a paragraph of descriptive text instead of a genus-species designation. Quaint and still scientifically valuable, but not very searchable. We've come a long way.

HELPING HOME GARDENERS grow—and eat—local since 1991! Long before the William T. Kemper Center for Home Gardening display gardens appeared on the scene, the Garden contained several displays of "economic" plants, including for many years, hemp.

THE NATIONAL HISTORIC
Landmark designation,
given in 1977, is the highest
honor awarded by the U.S.
Department of the Interior.
There are only 13 in St. Louis.

IN 1859, THE SAME YEAR THE MISSOURI BOTANICAL GARDEN
opened to the public, Charles Darwin published the foundation
of evolutionary biology, *On the Origin of Species*. Since then,
the Garden has become a world leader in botanical systematics,
the study of plants and their evolutionary relationships.
Darwiniana in the Garden's collections include first editions
of *On the Origin* and a dried fern collected in 1834 during the
voyage of the *Beagle*.

PLANTS OF THE BIBLE inside the Shoenberg Temperate House. Shaw loved plants, and in them, saw evidence of the Divine. In his will, he provided for the annual preaching of a sermon at Christ Church Cathedral on "the wisdom and goodness of God, as shown in the growth of flowers, fruits, and other products of the vegetable kingdom." During his lifetime, he published a slender reference volume on *Plants of the Bible*.

INDIANA BANANA IS BUT ONE OF THE MANY
common names given this unusual native
fruit, the pawpaw. Its genus (*Asimina*) is the
only member of the custard apple family that
lives outside the tropics (seen here in the
Doris I. Schnuck Children's Garden). Fruits
appear in August/September, and may be
substituted for banana in baking recipes.

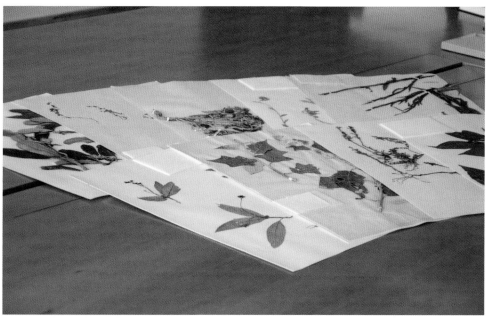

EX HERBARIO MUSEI BRITANNICI

PLANTS OF
CAPTAIN COOK'S FIRST VOYAGE
1768-1771

Grewia crenata (Forst.) Schinz & Guillaumin

SOCIETY ISLANDS

1769

Coll. JOSEPH BANKS & DANIEL SOLANDER

BANKS AND SOLANDER PLANT SPECIMENS.
Daniel Solander was one of Linnaeus's apostles
who went out into the world as a "species
seeker." He teamed up with British botanist
Joseph Banks to travel to the South Pacific
aboard Captain Cook's *Endeavour* between
1768 and 1771. They would be among the
first Europeans to set foot on Australia. Cook
named Sydney's harbor "Botany Bay" in honor
of the many plants they collected there. More
than 44 of these original collections are in the
Missouri Botanical Garden Herbarium.

DONNA HERRERA HOLDS WHAT IS BELIEVED TO BE THE OLDEST SPECIMEN in the Missouri Botanical Garden Herbarium. The Garden's Herbarium has over 6.5 million items. Catalogers are working daily to enter all the collections into the database, but they still encounter surprises. In 2015, Herrera was cataloging a cache of specimens from the original Bernhardi Herbarium (see page 113) when a label caught her eye: *Anemone vernalis* from Gdansk, Poland, collected by Jacob Breyne in 1692. That's nearly 40 years prior to what was previously believed to be the oldest specimen in the collection.

THESE TWIN CLEAVER-BROOKS LOW-PRESSURE, HOT-WATER boilers stand 10 feet tall and were lowered by crane through the window opening into the Boiler House in 1986. In the early 20th century, two high-pressure steam boilers literally filled this room; they were twice as big as the existing models. A full-time stationary engineer was required to monitor them. The Boiler House, located just to the northwest of the Emerson Electric Conservation Center, was built in 1911 to provide heat to the entire Garden. The accompanying underground coal bin was vast. Steam tunnels run underground all the way to Tower Grove House.

SIBTHORP'S *FLORA GRAECA* IS CONSIDERED A MASTERPIECE
of printing, engraving, color, and design. Its artist, Ferdinand
Bauer, is a peer of Redouté, but few have heard of him.
Published between 1804 and 1840, the series includes 10
oversized volumes detailing the plants of Greece and the
eastern Mediterranean. Production costs were so high that
only 30 sets were made. In 1830, the set cost £620, or today's
equivalent of $78,000. It is the most costly set of books devoted
to any flora. Its fame ushered in an era of increased public
interest in horticulture in Britain. Many pictured plants would
become perennials in temperate gardens.

SHAW NEVER MARRIED, BUT HE DID not lack for female friends. Effie Carstang became such a close friend that Shaw gave her a piano, or rather, loaned it, as he later claimed. She sued for breach of promise for the intent to marry—and won. The jury awarded Carstang $100,000, the largest sum ever in such an action at the time. The verdict came just as the Garden was opening; Shaw appealed the case and won in 1860, vacating the award. While the piano in Tower Grove House dates to the same era, and was also owned by Shaw, it was made by Allison & Allison of London. The piano in the lawsuit was made in Baltimore.

GARDEN BOTANIST DR. CARMEN ULLOA holding *Quipuanthus epipetricus*, the 6.5 millionth specimen in the Garden Herbarium. Many botanists will enjoy the chance to name a new species (over 130 by Garden scientists in 2014), but naming a new genus is considerably rarer. After genetic studies supported the designation of a new genus, the name came to Dr. Ulloa in a dream: "I woke up thinking the arrangement of fruits and flowers reminded me of a *quipu*." The *quipu* is an ancient record-keeping device of knots on strings used in the Andes, where the plant was found. Known from only two populations, *Q. epipetricus* is listed as endangered.

AMAZING MAIZE. THE GARDEN'S COLLECTION OF hundreds of cultivated varieties of corn shows the amazing evolution of teosinte to the crop we recognize today. Rarities include cobs collected from a 900-year-old Anasazi ruin in southern Colorado. The William L. Brown Center at the Garden is an international leader in ethnobotany, the study of plants and people. This includes working to document and preserve crop diversity. The Center also works to build scientific capacity in developing countries where the majority of the world's plant species exist.

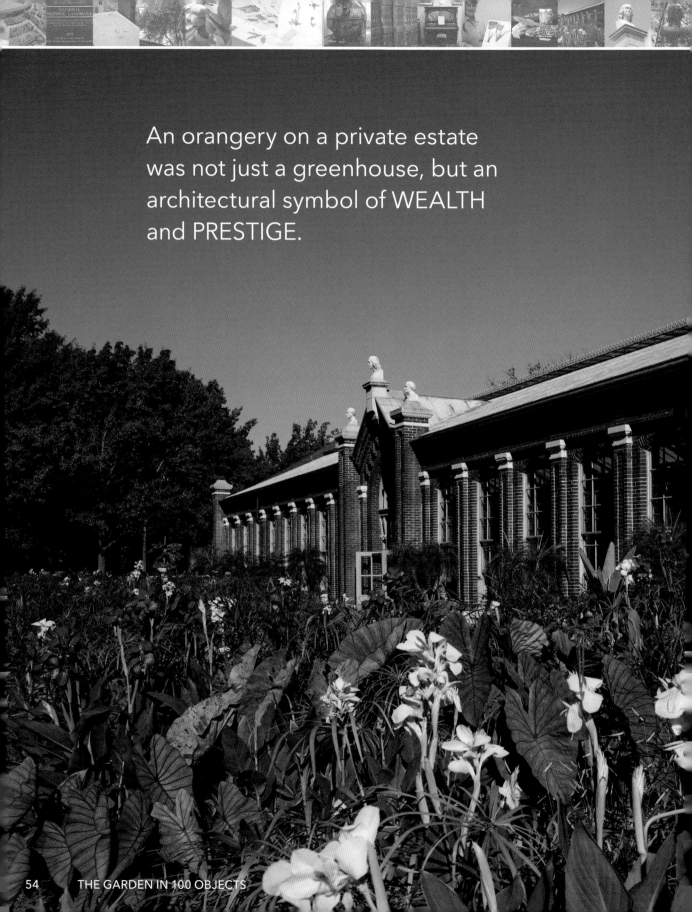

An orangery on a private estate was not just a greenhouse, but an architectural symbol of WEALTH and PRESTIGE.

CARL LINNAEUS, THREE views. Known as the "Prince of Nature" by his contemporaries, Carl Linnaeus was the botanist who simplified plant classification to genus and species. Through his charismatic teaching and writing, he inspired a generation of naturalists and plant hunters. The marble bust (1881) is installed atop the Linnean House, named in his honor. The bronze bust (1989) springs from the boughs of a Linden tree, the source of the name Linnaeus. From where the Garden received the plaster bust is a mystery.

NETS SAFELY CATCH
Osage orange fruits in the
Doris I. Schnuck Children's
Garden. These trees are
among the oldest at the
Garden. They appear as
an allée leading to Shaw's
country home in Compton &
Dry's 1875 *Pictorial St. Louis*.
Native to the region, the tree
has softball-sized fruits that
perhaps evolved for dispersal
by now extinct megafauna,
such as wooly mammoths and
giant ground sloths.

THE TOM K. SMITH GAZEBO in the Cherbonnier English Woodland Garden is one of many magical hideaways that delight visitors to the Garden.

SHAW'S HANDWRITTEN GUIDE TO HIS GARDEN, 1880. HE wrote: "Of all public resorts a scientific garden, when properly kept, will be found to be not only one of the most delightful mediums for intellectual gratification and amusement, but, also one of the greatest temporal blessings that can be enjoyed by a people." Amen.

JUST AS A GARDEN IS ALWAYS A WORK IN PROGRESS, SO TOO the guidebook. Shaw's original handwritten guide to the Garden never saw publication, but established the template for future editions. The Garden published its first formal guidebook in 1893, with new editions arriving every 10 years or so thereafter. The date in the book is a library stamp from 1908.

JESUP COLLECTION OF NORTH AMERICAN FORESTRY
cabinet, 1880s. Morris Ketchum Jesup was a wealthy financier
who retired in 1884 and devoted himself to philanthropy.
One of his many interests was the American forest, which was
rapidly being logged. He funded the Jesup Collection of North
American Woods at the American Museum of Natural History
and sold cabinets filled with cards of wood samples. The
Missouri Botanical Garden collection is believed to be one of
the most complete sets in existence.

TIBETAN YAK-BUTTER TEA SERVICE MADE OF rhododendron wood with drinking bowls and lidded storage dishes for butter and roasted barley flour (*tsampa*, a dietary staple). Changes in the climate are already having a visible impact in the Tibetan plateau and other high-elevation mountainous regions throughout the world. Garden researchers are documenting changes in alpine flora, and the traditional cultures these plants support. The loss of glaciers and permanent snows has cosmic implications for some of these cultures: "If the snow disappears, people will disappear from the Earth," one Tibetan man told them.

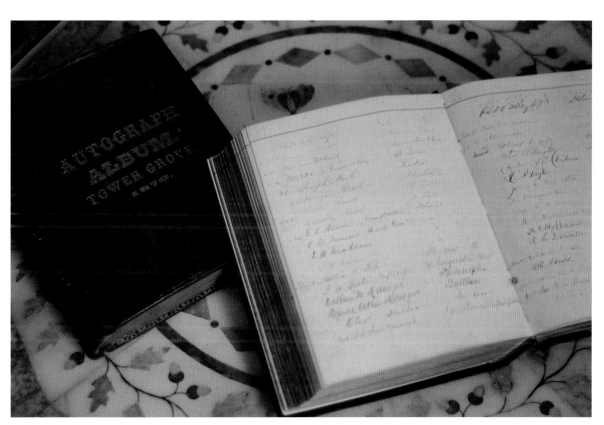

"VISITORS TO TOWER GROVE AND THE BOTANICAL GARDEN are respectfully requested to write their names." Over the 50 years these books were kept (1858–1909), a wide range of visitors signed the book: General Ulysses S. Grant, General Custer and his wife, P.T. Barnum, and perhaps most notably, Oscar Wilde (signature at top right).

"FOR SOME TIME PAST, IT HAS SEEMED TO ME THAT MY library of early botanical literature would be more used at the Mo. Bot. Garden than elsewhere." When he wrote this donation letter in 1892, agricultural scientist E. Lewis Sturtevant had assembled one of the most comprehensive reference collections of his era, including nearly 500 rare pre-Linnean books. The Sturtevant gift confirmed the position of what is now the Peter H. Raven Library as one of the world's best botanical libraries.

THE ZIMMERMAN SENSORY GARDEN features plants and artwork for the visually impaired. *Bell Tree* is a hands-on sculpture and a perennial favorite with children of all ages. The bronze bells are by sculptor Paolo Soleri, who studied with Frank Lloyd Wright and established Arcosanti, an "experimental town" in the Arizona desert. (opposite)

TROPICAL WATER LILIES are seen throughout the country in parks and botanical gardens. They have become so commonly displayed thanks in large part to propagation methods developed at the Missouri Botanical Garden. The Garden's head of horticulture in the early 20th century, George H. Pring, was a national expert and breeder of water lilies. Many of his *Nymphaea* are named for family and co-workers and are still popular in commerce today.

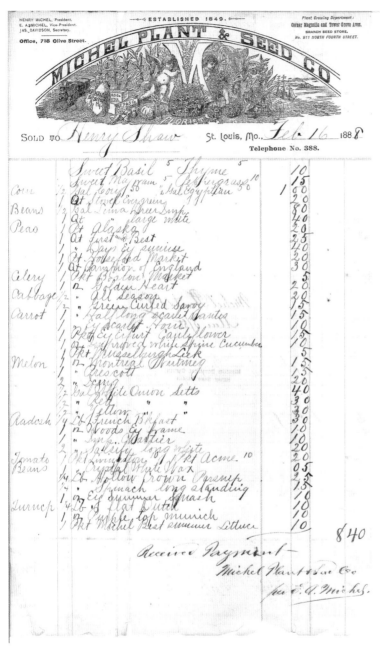

IN SHAW'S DAY, THE BOTANICAL GARDEN OPEN TO THE public was north of Tower Grove House. To the south and southwest was private property, including an area called "the farm," where he raised livestock and crops for his own table. This receipt from 1888 is notable for the variety of what we would now call heirloom vegetables, such as Golden Heart celery and Scarlet Nantes carrot.

AN ANCIENT AND UNUSUAL TREE, *GINKGO BILOBA* IS CONSIDERED A LIVING fossil. It is dioecious, which is to say, male and female organs occur on different trees. Nowadays, U.S. nurseries sell male plants almost exclusively. (The females produce fleshy seeds that produce stinky butyric acid as they decay.) This old ginkgo just north of the Cleveland Avenue Gatehouse is special: it's a male tree with one female branch, making it officially bisexual. See if you can spot the fruits in late spring on a west-southwestern branch about thirty feet up.

DRACAENA UMBRACULIFERA in the Climatron. Not seen in the wild for 200 years, and therefore believed extinct, this umbrella dracaena tree was part of a planned program to repopulate the island of Mauritius, where it was believed to originate. However, a cutting-edge genetic comparison of all 17 known *D. umbraculifera* in the world revealed a different source entirely: Madagascar. Garden staff went looking for it there and found it in the wild. It is still critically endangered... though not extinct.

THE RAREST WORK FROM THE GARDEN'S rare book collection: *Les liliacées* ("the Lily family") by Pierre-Joseph Redouté, published from 1802 to 1816. Nicknamed "the Raphael of flowers," the Flemish artist Redouté was the most celebrated botanical illustrator of his day. The Empress Joséphine Napoléon was his patron when he undertook this eight-volume, 486-engraving work. Only two other copies are known to exist that show the black-and-white plate strikes alongside the hand-colored completed illustrations.

The sign in the image reads:

Parsley, Sage, Rosemary, and Thyme Stuffing

Herbs & Spices
Garlic | *Allium sativum*
Italian (flat-leaf) parsley | *Petroselinum crispum var. neopolitanum*
Black pepper | *Piper nigrum*
Rosemary | *Rosmarinus officinalis*
Sage leaves | *Salvia officinalis*
Thyme | *Thymus vulgaris*

Vegetables
Vegetables and ... le broth
Carrots | *Dauc...*
Celery | *Apium...*
Onions | *Alliu...*

Dry Ingredients
Bread Crumbs
→ Common wheat | *Triticum aestivum*
→ Sugar (sugarcane | *Saccharum officinarum*)

Liquids
Extra virgin olive oil (olive | *Olea europaea*)
Vegan butter
→ Palm oil (oil palm | *Elaeis guineenis*)
→ Canola oil (rapeseed | *Brassica napus*)
→ Soybean oil (soybean | *Glycine max*)
→ Flax oil (flax | *Linum usitatissimum*)
→ Olive oil (olive | *Olea europaea*)

Italian parsley,
*Petroselinum crispum
var. neopolitanum*

Cook this one at home!
for a complete listing of reci... ...www.stlouisherbsociety.com
...ne St. Louis Herb Society.

Chives
Allium schoenop...
Alliaceae
Balkens, Siberia, ...

HISTORY MEETS HIGH-TECH. THE ST. LOUIS HERB SOCIETY, established 1941, is one of the longest serving plant societies affiliated with the Garden. Among their many fine contributions are these attractive new container gardens. Each pot contains the herbs for a specific recipe. Visitors are invited to scan the QR code to find the full information online.

CATTLEYA LABIATA BY BRITISH ARTIST MARGARET MEE. The Garden has a collection of eight original Mee watercolors of Amazonian orchids. Mee is famed for her studies of Amazon rainforest flora. She is equally famous as an early environmentalist. Over 30 years, starting in 1956, she documented the beauty of the Amazon—and then sounded the alarm about its destruction due to mining and deforestation. (opposite)

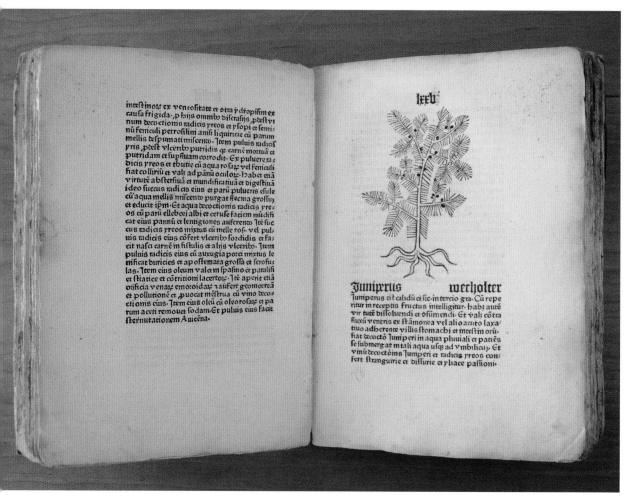

THE EARLIEST ILLUSTRATED BOOK FROM THE Garden's rare book collection: a Latin herbal with woodcut block illustrations, from 1484. Herbals are some of the earliest information ever recorded. They contain descriptions of plants and their traditional medicinal uses— incredibly important at a time when almost all medicines derived from plants. Grants from the National Institutes of Health and the Food and Drug Administration help the Garden continue research into medicinal plants today.

TAIHU STONE IN THE MARGARET GRIGG-NANJING FRIENDSHIP GARDEN donated by former Garden president Dr. Peter H. Raven. Rocks are essential features in Chinese gardens. Stones that have been sculpted by erosion or other natural forces, such as this piece of porous limestone from Lake Tai, are especially prized. They are thought to embody the dynamic forces of nature.

HENRY SHAW'S ORIGINAL MEDICINE CHEST is filled with plant extracts: "Syrup of Squills, Syrup of Rhubarb, Tincture of Lavender, Powdered Ipecacuanha, Powdered Jalap, Castor Oil, Essence of Peppermint, Laudanum," among others. Today, though we might not always recognize it, many of our prescription medicines derive directly from plants. New medicines may be derived from plant diversity in the future, which is essential to preserve.

IN VICTORIAN STYLE, SHAW PLANNED HIS OWN FINAL resting place. He commissioned his architect George I. Barnett in 1885 to design the copper-roofed octagonal mausoleum in rose granite. Baron Ferdinand von Miller II sculpted the white marble statue of Shaw in repose. Shaw has the original photograph upon which it is based taken while he was very much alive and able to approve the artist's handiwork.

Nine bean-rows will I have there,
a hive for the honey-bee,

And live alone in the bee-loud glade.

—W. B. Yeats

HONEYBEES POLLINATE MANY OF OUR FOOD CROPS. THEY
are disappearing in unheard-of numbers due to a complex web
of pressures, including disease, pesticides, mites, and extreme
weather linked to climate change. The Kemper Center for Home
Gardening demonstration gardens offer an example of hive
management, while helping ensure the pollination of Garden
fruits and flowers.

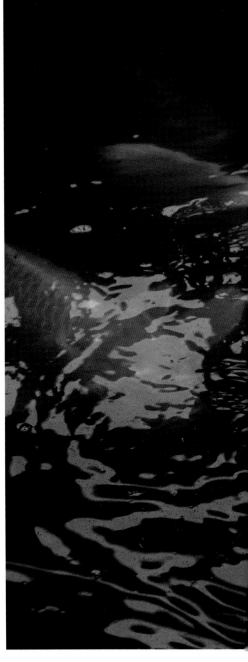

THIS RESTORATION-ERA LEAD CISTERN DATES TO 1668 during the reign of England's Merry Monarch, King Charles II. It is frequently mistaken as a monument of some kind in the Hosta Garden. However, in its time, it would have stood near the base of a downspout beside a building, likely in London. The top was added upon its installation at the Garden to prevent standing water breeding mosquitoes.

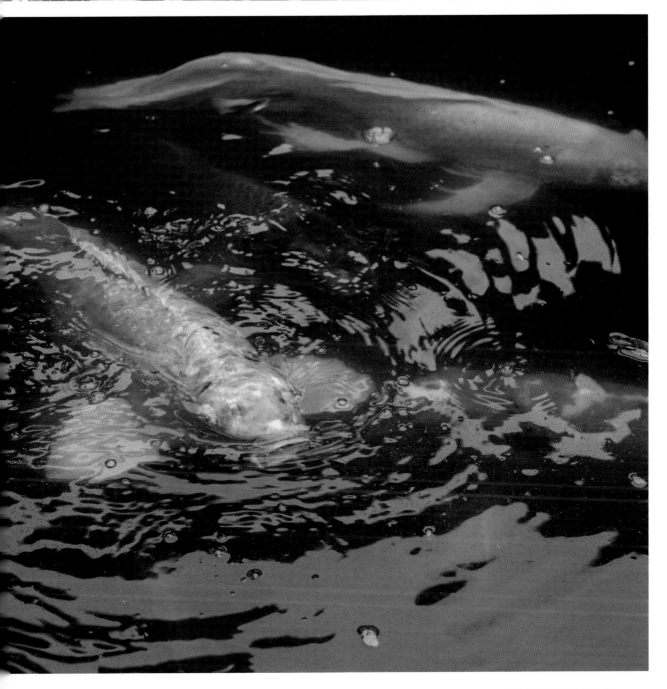

KOI ARE THE ORNAMENTAL CARP FAVORED IN JAPANESE gardens. Varieties are distinguished by color and pattern, with some rare varieties fetching significant sums. In Japanese, *koi* is a homophone for a word meaning "affection," and the fish are symbols of love and friendship in Japan. *Koinobori*, or carp streamers, are traditionally flown on Children's Day, May 5.

CRANE ISLAND, ORIGINAL ARTWORK BY KOICHI KAWANA.
Kawana was the Japanese-American architect of *Seiwa-en*
(the Japanese Garden). In addition to conceptual drawings,
he would often do ink washes and watercolors of gardens he
designed before they were built. "His drawings today help us
gain insight into his vision," says Horticulture Supervisor Ben
Chu. "For example, how he felt the pines should lean, and how
the pines should show off their structure."

"WE HAVE RELATIVELY SHORT LIVES, AND YET BY PRESERVING the world in a condition that is worthy of us, we win a kind of immortality. We become stewards of the Earth." The Garden's six previous Directors/Presidents, and the year they started, top row, from left: William Trelease (1889), George T. Moore (1912), Edgar S. Anderson (1954); second row, from left: Frits Went (1958), David Gates (1965), and Peter H. Raven (1971).

HENRY SHAW GESTURES TO VISITORS TO SIT AND REST
for a moment. The ornate bench by Paul Granlund is composed
of grapevines, reflecting Shaw's love of viticulture and wine.
"Historically and physiologically the use of good wine produced
those great and luminous developments of the human mind,"
wrote Shaw, "Which at diverse epochs and always progressively
have drawn the world to regions of a better civilization."

"CATAWBA AND NORTON'S Virginia," wrote Shaw, "are generally considered the best grapes for wine making in Missouri." Shaw enjoyed wine and grew wine grapes on the grounds. That tradition continues today in the research vineyard at the Kemper Center for Home Gardening. The fact that we can enjoy imported wine as well owes thanks to Shaw's botanical advisor George Engelmann. In the 1870s, French vines were under attack by the insect *Phylloxera*. Engelmann knew a wild vine of the Mississippi Valley (*Vitis riparia*) that was resistant to *Phylloxera* and would not cross-pollinate with less resistant species. He arranged to send millions of shoots and seeds to France. Voilà! Crisis averted.

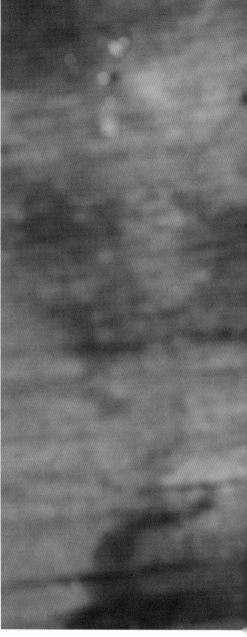

SHAW'S UNCLE WILLIAM HOOLE WAS THE MAKER OF THIS decorative barometer. The Hooles were a well-to-do manufacturing family, of which Shaw's mother was a member. Shaw's success in business owed to his own flinty bargaining abilities, but also to his family connections for importing. One can imagine Shaw checking his barometer daily at the country house and recording the weather. He apparently enjoyed record keeping, based on the cabinet-full of ledgers he left behind.

MAMMILLARIA HERRERAE FROM THE Garden's cactus collection. Native to Querétaro, Mexico, the cactus is critically endangered by illegal collecting. According to the International Union for Conservation of Nature (IUCN), commercial and amateur collectors have nearly stripped the site where it grows. Botanical gardens must preserve some plants *ex situ* (away from the site), while working to preserve habitat whenever possible. Many unusual specimens from the Garden's cactus and succulent collection can be seen in the Linnean House in a rotating display.

Yours truly Ths Nuttall 1859

ADR. DE JUSSIEU 1844

LINNÆUS.

THESE PORTRAITS ONCE HUNG from the second-story catwalk in the Museum Building (see photo page 19). Shaw commissioned them from three different artists in the 1870s. (Perhaps he was impatient. He did the same thing in Tower Grove Park, commissioning three different sculptors to craft busts of composers in the 1880s). With the exception of Shaw's scientific advisor George Engelmann and Asa Gray of Harvard, the paintings are botanists associated with 19th century European botanical gardens.

They are (L–R): Asa Gray, Thomas Nuttall, François André Michaux, George Engelmann (painter: Rollin A. Clifford); Pierre Magnol, Antoine-Laurent de Jussieu, Karl von Linné (Linnaeus), John Lindley (painter: Ettore S. Miragoli); Joseph Pitton de Tournefort, Augustin-Pyramus de Candolle (painter: Oscar Hallwig)

OVER THE YEARS TRAMS HAVE TRANSPORTED VISITORS across the 79-acre expanse of the Garden. More recently they have been employed as part of the Garden's float in the annual St. Patrick's Day parade in downtown St. Louis. A tram dubbed Daffy O'Dill was specially decorated for the occasion and gets the honor of pulling the float every year. Garden president Dr. Peter Wyse Jackson has participated every year, even serving as Honorary Parade Marshal in 2013.

"I WAS A YOUNG BOTANIST IN 1985 WHEN I EMBARKED upon my first-ever tropical expedition to the Indian Ocean island of Mauritius. One of the most fascinating plants I encountered there was the Round Island bottle palm (*Hyophorbe lagenicaulis*), which has been saved from extinction by being cultivated in tropical gardens worldwide. In the wild, however, fewer than ten mature plants survive. Whenever I encounter these old friends, I greet them with a hug."

—Dr. Peter Wyse Jackson, President of the Missouri Botanical Garden (opposite)

GEORGE ENGELMANN, THREE VIEWS: self-portrait in pencil as a young man, circa 1830; daguerreotype by Thomas Easterly, circa 1850s, with wife Dorothea Horstmann and their only child, George Julius Engelmann (who would one day become a noted gynecologist); maquette for the Garden's bronze bust by Paul Granlund (2000). When Dr. George Engelmann emigrated from his native Germany to the American frontier town of St. Louis in the 1830s, he brought with him a lifelong love of botany. While working as a physician, he also became Shaw's scientific advisor, and is credited with establishing the Garden's serious botanical research enterprise.

OSBORNE 1 COMPUTER, CIRCA 1981, used to develop Tropicos. In the late 1970s, young Garden PhD Robert Magill assayed computer programming, teaching himself CBASIC. He used it to create one of the world's first plant databases, Tropicos. Magill recounts lugging this Osborne 1 (weight: 25 lbs.) to governmental agencies across Washington D.C. with fellow researcher Marshall Crosby to promote the use of computers in plant research. Did they secure any grant money? "We were ahead of our time!" Today, tropicos.org is freely available on the web and contains an astonishing 1.2 million plant names.

CAMELLIAS HAVE BLOOMED in the Linnean House since 1919, but have grown in tea cultivation for over 2,000 years. Recently, cultivars have been bred to survive colder outdoor temperatures (examples can be seen in the English Woodland Garden.) "Tea…will always be the favorite beverage of the intellectual," wrote De Quincey. True to his English roots, Shaw took tea in the afternoons.

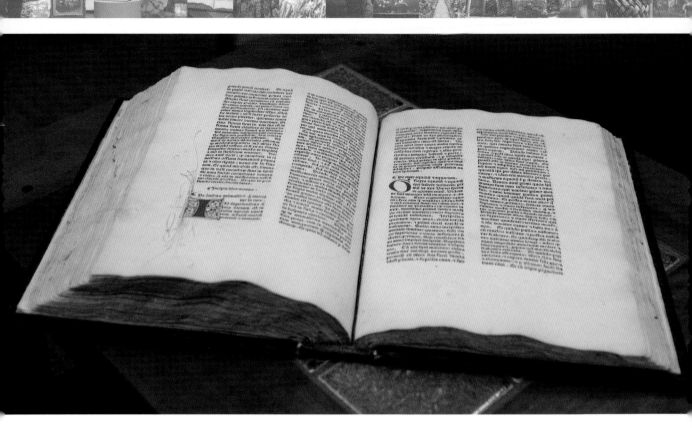

THE OLDEST VOLUME IN THE GARDEN'S RARE BOOK collection: the *Opus ruralium commodorum* ("book of rural benefits"), printed in 1474. A runaway best seller of the late Middle Ages, *Opus ruralium* was the first modern printed text on agriculture, a popular subject in an era racked by repeat famines. An estimated 57 editions were produced in a variety of languages, and it stayed in print for over a century.

A NATIONAL CHAMPION! THIS WHITE BASSWOOD (*TILIA americana* var. *heterophylla*) is the largest known tree of this species in the U.S.. On the National Register of Big Trees, it is listed as 103 feet tall (in a species that normally tops out at 90 feet). It was cored in 2008 and found to date to circa 1925, making it 90 years old. A native Linden, the name "basswood" refers to the tree's inner bark—or *bast*—from which a strong fiber is produced. (opposite)

"There is nothing in the world half so beautiful as the gardener's work. What are jewelers, or watchmakers, or ivory carvers, or even painters to compare with a genuine Gardener? The things that they handle are dead and cannot know the treatment they receive. But our work is living and natural, and knows us, and adapts itself to following our desires and pleasures. It has its own tempers, and moods of feeling, the same that we have; for every plant that lives is sensitive."

–From the Victorian novel *Christowell*, as quoted by Henry Shaw in his Garden guide.

MISCELLANEOUS DAFFODIL, *Narcissus* 'Tete-a-Tete', and common hyacinth, *Hyacinthus orientalis* 'Fondant', in the Heckman Bulb Garden.

LODOICEA MALDIVICA OR COCO-DE-MER IN THE CLIMATRON.
Native to the Seychelles Islands, Coco-de-Mer, or the double
coconut palm, produces the largest seed in the world, weighing
up to 60 pounds. Due to their astounding size and unusual
shape, the seeds are prized as art objects and talismans. Over-
collection has resulted in diminished reproduction, and the
palm is now threatened. It is unknown if the Garden's specimen
growing in the Climatron is male or female, as it has not
bloomed yet, but a sample seed is on display at the Garden.

PAINTED VASCULUM, 1890S. A VASCULUM (FROM THE LATIN diminutive of *vas* or vessel) was a flattened metal cylinder with shoulder strap used in plant collecting. Botanists would line it with dampened paper to keep the samples fresh. Today, researchers use plastic bags for this purpose—more practical, but certainly less aesthetically pleasing.

CANARY IN THE COALMINE? IN 1926, THE GARDEN MOVED the orchid collection to Gray Summit away from the coal smoke in St. Louis. Thanks to antipollution measures, the orchid collection was able to move back in 1958. Today, the Garden's orchid collection may be indicating climate change: some varieties used for years in the Garden's Orchid Show in February are now blooming too early to be show-worthy. (overleaf)

Wake! For the Sun behind yon Eastern height

Has chased the Session of the Stars from Night;

And to the field of Heav'n ascending, strikes

The Sultan's Turret with a Shaft of Light.

-*Rubaiyat* of Omar Kayyam

THIS ORNATELY CARVED chair sits on the patio under a wooden arbor, or *chardak*, in the Edward L. Bakewell Ottoman Garden.

HALLOWED GROUND.
Visitors may walk on Teahouse Island once a year, during Japanese Festival. (Tickets are limited.) The teahouse was a gift from Missouri's sister state of Nagano, Japan. A *soan*, or "farm hut" style, it was built in Japan, then reassembled here by Japanese craftsmen and blessed by a Shinto priest.

THIS DECORATIVE ORNAMENT IS WOVEN from vanilla beans, several dozen of them. After saffron, vanilla is the second most expensive spice in the world. A single bean retails today for around five dollars in the U.S.. But in Madagascar, where over half the world's vanilla is grown, farmers receive only pennies. Some create crafts out of the pods, such as this woven ornament, in hopes of generating more income. The Garden's program in Madagascar works not only to preserve plants and their habitats and teach conservation, but also to raise the standard of living for Malagasy people.

THE KEMPER CENTER FOR HOME GARDENING WELCOMES you! Since 1991, visitors have been able to seek help from Master Gardener "plant doctors," check out the houseplant displays, and research all kinds of gardening-related topics in the reference area. It's also a favorite retreat from hot or cold weather in the Garden, especially when the Terrace Café is open. (opposite)

ITALIAN RURAL SCENE BY FILIPPO PALIZZI, CIRCA
1870s, hanging in the Garden President's office. Palizzi lived in
Naples and is associated with the Italian *Verismo*, or "realism"
school, a precursor to French Impressionism. The painting was
donated in 1966 by descendants of William H. H. Pettus, one of
the Garden's original Trustees selected by Shaw.

"IF THEREFORE ANY BE desirous to keepe this tree, he must so provide for it, that it be preserved from any cold, either in the winter of spring, and exposed to the comfort of the sunne in summer. And for that purpose, some keepe them in great square boxes, and lift them to and fro by iron hooks on the sides, or cause them to be rowled by trundels, or small wheeles under them, to place them in a house or close gallerie for the winter time."

From the Garden's rare book collection, *Paradisi in sole paradisus terrestris*, or, *A garden of all sorts* by John Parkinson (London: 1629).

IN KEEPING WITH ITS original purpose as an orangery, the Linnean House displays potted citrus plants from fall through spring. In the summer months, these plants can be found throughout the Lichtenstein Victorian District.

THE GARDEN'S FIRST ORCHID SHOW WAS held in 1924. Throughout the early part of the century, the Garden was at the forefront of orchid collection and propagation. During the First World War, the Garden's collection was so renowned that the Garden obtained a special permit to burn coal to heat the orchid greenhouse. Orchids from the Garden were used to make the bouquet for the "Queen of Love and Beauty" at the annual Veiled Prophet ball in the 1920s and '30s.

Leipzig, Saxony, December 18th 1857

Mr Henry Shaw at St Louis
to Theodor Bernhardi, agent

to the Herbarium or Collection of Plants
of the late Prof Joh. Jac. Bernhardi
of Erfurt, consisting of 374 packages
(said to contain about 40000 species)
of dried plants — — — Rixdollars 400.—

Recd. Payt. by Dr George Engelmann

Theodor Bernhardi

THIS SIMPLE HANDWRITTEN RECEIPT MARKS THE BEGINNING of the Garden's internationally renowned herbarium. In 1857, Shaw's scientific advisor George Engelmann arranged the purchase of the "Bernhardi Herbarium," a collection of roughly 60,000 specimens assembled by Johann Jakob Bernhardi, a German doctor and botany enthusiast. Today, the Garden's Herbarium has grown to more than 6.5 million specimens.

MOST PEOPLE ASSOCIATE TULIPS WITH HOLLAND, BUT THE bulbs that inspired the 17th century "tulipomania" were imported from the Ottoman Empire. Visitors to the Bakewell Ottoman Garden in spring are treated to a collection of rare and historic hybrid tulips. (overleaf)

ORIGINAL ENCAUSTIC TILES
line the first floor of Shaw's
town house and the Museum
Building. Though known
for his modest ways, Shaw
liked nice things. These
richly colored and patterned
beauties are known as
Minton tiles, manufactured
by Minton, Hollins and
Company in Staffordshire,
England. The firm's tiles won
numerous gold medals at
international exhibitions and
were considered the best tiles
made. An elaborate suite of
Mintons would be installed
just a few years later at the U.S.
Capitol Building in 1856.

FROM LEONARD SENCE OF NEW YORK, "EXCLUSIVE IMPORTER OF variegated Pyrennian marble," Shaw commissioned beautiful stone mantelpieces for both his city and country homes, but none so beautiful as that found in the second floor of his town house. Carved of Carrara, the mantel features a central monogram (HS) flanked on either corner by draped cherubs, ropes of fruits and flowers, and architectural details. During many of the years since Shaw's death, this room has been used as the President's office.

She walks in beauty, like the night.

SHAW NEVER MARRIED, NOR DID HE LEAVE ANY RECORD OF his feelings about love and attraction. Nonetheless, we can read between the lines from his handwritten comments in his travel journals about the various "beauties," "coquettes," and "fair damsels" he espied in towns throughout Europe. He apparently purchased this painting on his first trip abroad. The artist and subject are unknown, but it is recorded in an inventory of his possessions as "Venetian lady" hanging in Tower Grove House.

CYCADS IN THE CLIMATRON.
Although they may look like palms, cycads are actually cone-bearing plants from the age of the dinosaurs. Their tough leathery leaves and thorns ward off all but the toughest herbivores. They are among the oldest plants known— and they live for a long time too. Some of the Garden's cycads were exhibited at the 1904 World's Fair. Cycads are slow-growing, and many of them are vulnerable in the wild, often brought to the verge of extinction by over-collecting or habitat loss.

THE WHITMIRE WILDFLOWER GARDEN AT SHAW NATURE Reserve started as a birthday present from Blanton Whitmire to his wife Peg. Today over 800 species of native Missouri plants are on display.

THE WETLAND AT SHAW NATURE RESERVE IS THIRTY-TWO acres of seasonally flooded pools, marsh, wet prairie, and moist woodlands, watered by rainfall runoff from the prairie uplands nearby. Wetlands are the link between land and water. They are some of the earth's most productive ecosystems, and a great place for observing native flora and fauna. (opposite)

AT A 1905 MEETING,
the Garden's Board of Trustees
decided the Garden did not
own an impressive enough
likeness of Henry Shaw. They
commissioned the young
Richard E. Miller, who was
then emerging as a leading
American impressionist. The
result was a larger-than-life,
eight-foot-tall figure of a
slightly smiling Shaw with top
hat and walking stick. Today,
the painting hangs in the town
house, at the northern end
of the Garden's Shoenberg
Administration Building.

ARTIFACT KNOWN AS "SHAW'S CURIO BOX," CIRCA EARLY
1800s. This box is purported to have been carved by the
young Henry Shaw "from timbers taken from the church in
which he was christened." Shaw grew up in Sheffield, the
center of England's cutlery industry. He would later make his
fortune running a general store in the 1820s and 30s importing
Sheffield knives and other implements to St. Louis to equip
settlers headed west.

SINCE THE GARDEN'S
Sophia M. Sachs Butterfly
House opened in 1998,
the tropical blue morpho
has been so popular it has
become an unofficial mascot.
Their iridescent wings dazzle
when open, but morphos
are quick and unpredictable
flyers, making them difficult
to photograph. They are
territorial and are commonly
seen chasing each other
through the conservatory.
The Butterfly House is helping
to conserve areas in Costa
Rica where blue morphos
roam through a partnership
with El Bosque Nuevo.

'Tis the last rose of summer,

Left blooming alone;

All her lovely companions

Are faded and gone...

ROSA CHINENSIS 'OLD BLUSH' IN THE GLADNEY ROSE
Garden, a cutting of the actual "Last Rose of Summer." In 1805,
Irish poet Thomas Moore composed the poem, later set to
music, after spotting a late-blooming flower at Jenkinstown
House in County Kilkenny. A cutting of the rose was given
120 years later to Lois Wyse Jackson. Her son, Garden
President Dr. Peter Wyse Jackson, brought another with him
from Ireland to St. Louis.